Sand

or, Once Upon a Time in the Jazz Age

Written by Douglas Brode

Illustrated by Rose Mary Moziak

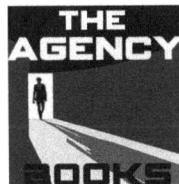

THE AGENCY BOOKS

an imprint of Sunbury Press, Inc.
Mechanicsburg, PA USA

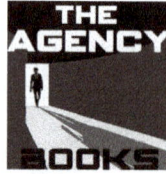

an imprint of Sunbury Press, Inc.
Mechanicsburg, PA USA

For information about special discounts for bulk purchases, please contact Sunbury Press Orders Dept. at (855) 338-8359 or orders@sunburypress.com.

To request one of our authors for speaking engagements or book signings, please contact Sunbury Press Publicity Dept. at publicity@sunburypress.com.

FIRST AGENCY BOOKS EDITION: March 2021

Interior design by Crystal Devine | Cover and Illustrations by Rose Mary Moziak | Edited by Douglas Brode.

Publisher's Cataloging-in-Publication Data
Names: Brode, Douglas, author | Moziak, Rose Mary, illustrator.
Title: Sand : or, once upon a time in the jazz age / Written by Douglas Brode Illustrated by Rose Mary Moziak.
Description: First trade paperback edition. | Mechanicsburg, PA : The Agency Books, 2021.
Summary: The birth of the roaring twenties, as young gossip columnist Louella Parsons and aged sportswriter Bat Masterson meet to cover the 'fight of the century' in which contender Jack Dempsey hopes to become the next heavyweight champion of the world.
Identifiers: ISBN : 978-1-620067-66-6 (softcover).
Subjects: FICTION / Historical.

Product of the United States of America
0 1 1 2 3 5 8 13 21 34 55

Continue the Enlightenment!

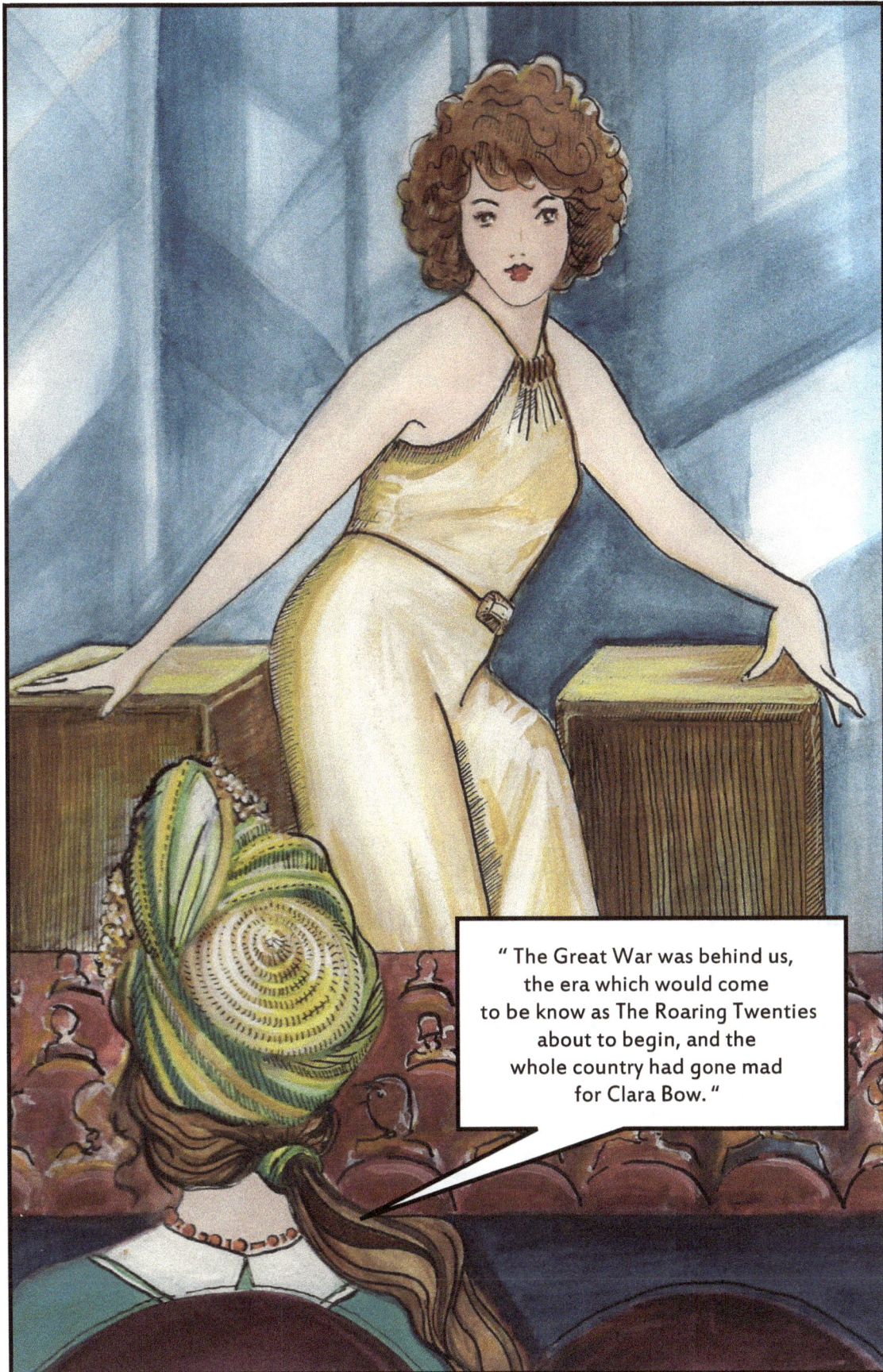

" The Great War was behind us, the era which would come to be know as The Roaring Twenties about to begin, and the whole country had gone mad for Clara Bow. "

2

I must have seemed a mere hayseed, because my editor,
Mr. William E. Lewis, had me writing obituaries and traffic accidents. "

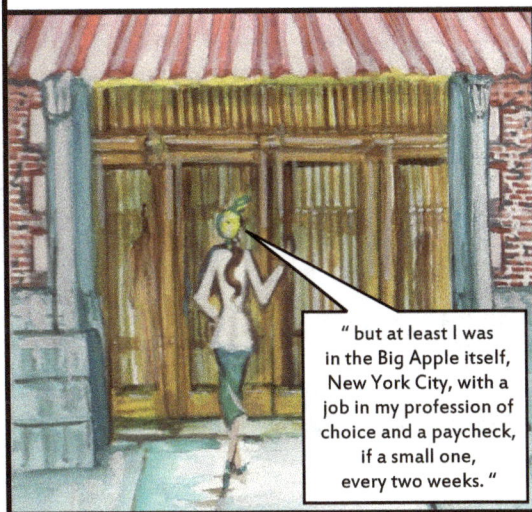

" but at least I was in the Big Apple itself, New York City, with a job in my profession of choice and a paycheck, if a small one, every two weeks. "

" Lou! Where have you been? Mr. Lewis wants you in his office IMMEDIATELY! "

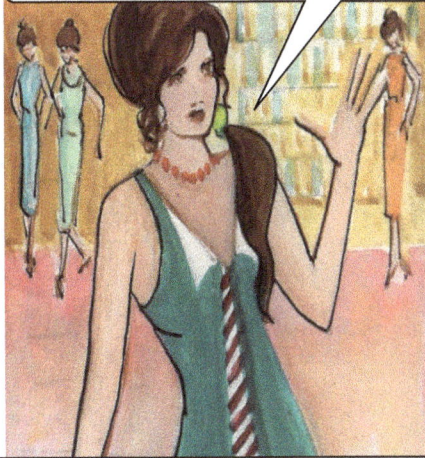

LOUELLA PARSONS
Gossip Columnist

" So instead of getting fired, I was promoted on the spot. Mr. Lewis figured that if his female employees cared so much about movie and sports stars, and the politicians and gangsters they associated with, then a column chronicling all the gossip would attract the new breed of women just then emerging to our paper. He later claimed that the " Morning Telegraph " was the first news venue in the country to feature a "gossip columnist, " a term he invented that very day. And I was it! "

"OVERNIGHT, I BECAME THE QUEEN OF MANHATTAN'S AFTER HOURS SCENE. A WEEK BEFORE, I'D BEEN UNABLE TO TALK MY WAY INTO THE CHIC CLUBS. NOW, THERE WAS A TABLE RESERVED FOR ME IN EACH OF THE HOT SPOTS, WHICH CAME TO BE REFERRED TO AS THE SPEAKEASIES."

"IT WORKED. CIRCULATION JUMPED! ALL OVER NEW YORK CITY, THE YOUNG WOMEN NOW KNOWN AS 'COSMOPOLITANS' READ MY COLUMN WITH THEIR MORNING COFFEE, BEFORE HEADING OUT INTO THE WORLD OF MEN THEY INVADED WHILE THE BOYS WERE ALL OVERSEAS ..."

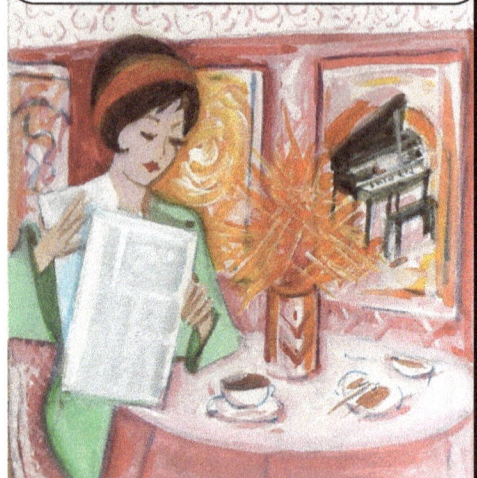

"WHEREVER SHE MIGHT WORK, LIKELY ATTENDING TO THE WHIMS OF OLDER WOMEN AND FANTASIZING ABOUT STEALING THAT GRAND DAME'S HANDSOME HUSBAND AWAY FOR HERSELF, SHE WOULD HAVE SOMETHING 'HOT' TO TALK ABOUT, THANKS TO ME."

"WHO WAS THELMA TODD DATING? WERE THE RUMORS ABOUT HER MOB LOVERS TRUE? AND WHAT HAD GONE WRONG WITH VILMA BANKY'S PROFESSIONAL AND PERSONAL LIFE?"

"THAT NIGHT, SHE'D BE OFF FOR AN EVENING ON THE TOWN, PERHAPS EVEN WITH THE HUSBAND OF THE WOMAN HE'D ATTENDED TO EARLIER THAT DAY. AFTER ALL, THE ERA THAT WOULD COME TO BE CALLED THE ROARING TWENTIES WAS JUST DAWNING. AND, AS COLE PORTER WOULD SOON SUM IT UP: ANYTHING GOES!

" The column became so popular that within two months, I had a half dozen of the brightest, most ambitious girls at the paper working for me full time. If you could call it work! Our ' job' was to hit all the hot night spots, flirt with the men until they loosened up and spilled all the beans that they were supposed to keep mum about. Then we'd arrive early in the morning to figure out some way to print just enough of the 'dirty' to tantalize the public without exposing our paper to a major law-suit. The whole process was kinda like solving a puzzle. And I love puzzles!

" What did I tell you, Bat? Like I said: " The Persian Garden of Cats."

" Reminds me of a den of pumas I stumbled into once, in New Mexico."

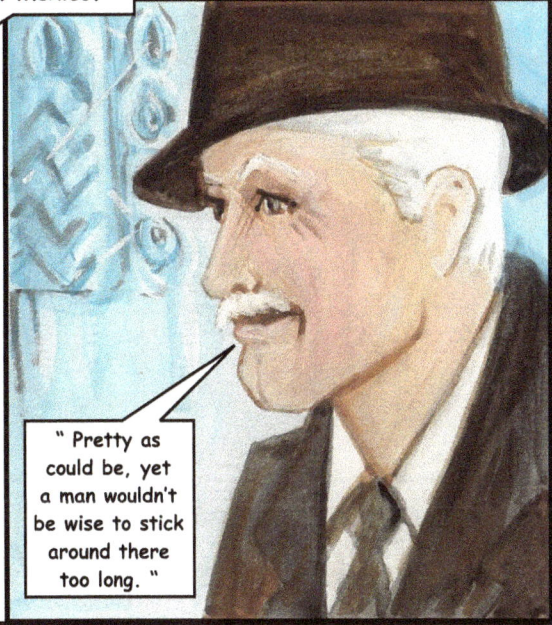

" Pretty as could be, yet a man wouldn't be wise to stick around there too long. "

"Why, that dapper old man had actually winked at me, if in a most charming manner."

"From the very first, I sensed that he was different from other men. How to describe his gait? Majestic!"

"Talk about nervy!"

"Who was that, Helen? The fellow with Mr. Lewis."

"Old Bat, the sportswritter. You've seen him around here before, haven't you?"

"I guess. Never really noticed him, though. You know I like 'em young."

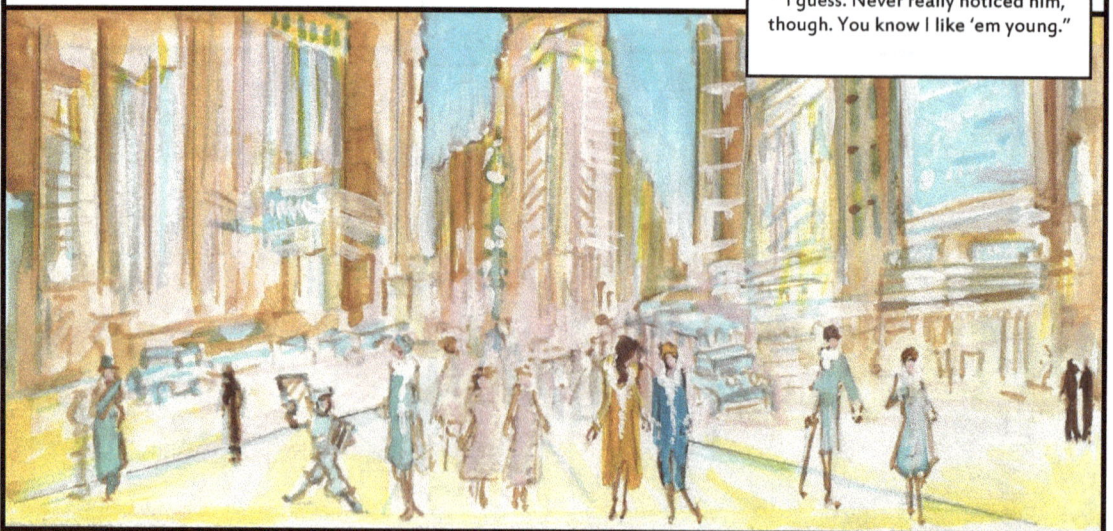

"The readership spiraled. I kept getting raises. Somehow, though, it was never enough. Always, I'd see new fashions I just had to have. And the car I'd purchased? Well, I'm too embarrassed to even say how much that set me back! So: By the third week of every month, I was flat broke. Me! The most sought-after girl in The Big Apple couldn't even afford to pay for her lunch."

10

Guess I was so locked into our contemporary cosmopolitan life, I didn't have any time for the past. Leastways, not 'til now.

WILLIAM BARCLAY MASTERSON
Sports Writer

I asked around and Helen was right. Why, I must've been the only person at the paper who'd never heard of Bat Masterson.

Ain't locked.

Anyway! Two days after Helen and I had talked, I finally worked up enough nerve to ...

Hello Mr. Masterson

" Bat "

Miss Parsons! This is a surprise!

A pleasant one, I hope.

You know, young lady that my name isn't Methusala.

That, I imagine, will depend on what you're here for.

My whole life in a room.

The last old-fashioned gentleman? Charming!

I hope when I reach your age, I've collected so many memories.

13

"AS I HEADED FOR THE DOOR, ALL AT ONCE A SICKLY SENSATION CAME OVER ME AND I FELT MYSELF FAINTING AWAY."
OOOOOOH!
MISS PARSONS? WHAT -
... IS IT?
FORGIVE ME. IT'S JUST THAT I ... HAVEN'T EATEN ALL DAY.

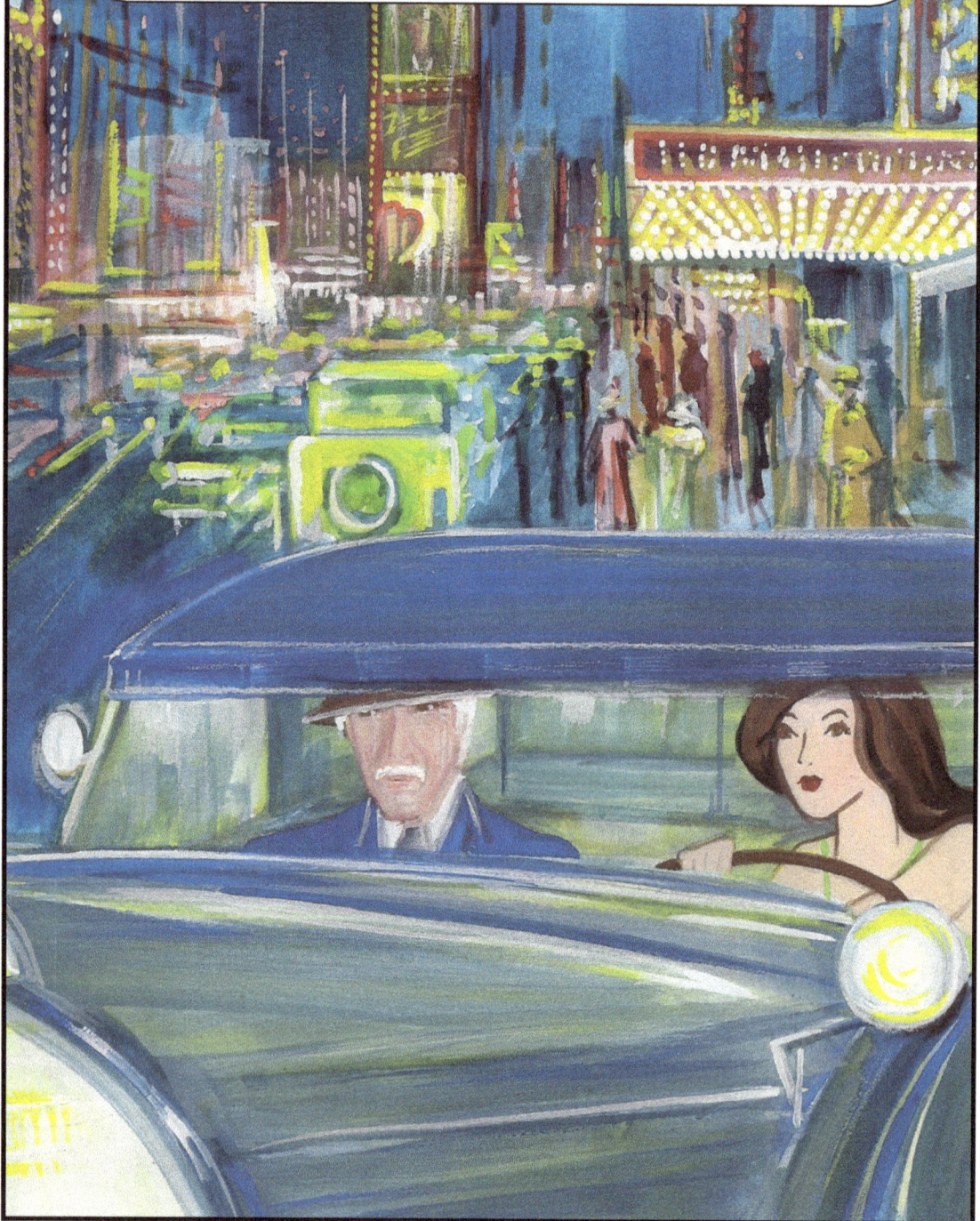

" I wasn't certain what "harbinger" meant, but I did get Bat's drift. At that moment, I realized, and for the first time, that I was more than just one more female reporter, if the lucky one who stumbled into a great job. Rather, I - Louella Parsons - was part and parcel of a new order of things. A new age as to morals and manners. For Bat, perhaps I was the symbol of the jazz age, as everyone was calling life in our time. Bat? For me? More than merely a man, Bat Masterson represented an America that had passed, the last vestige of some bygone, lost golden age."

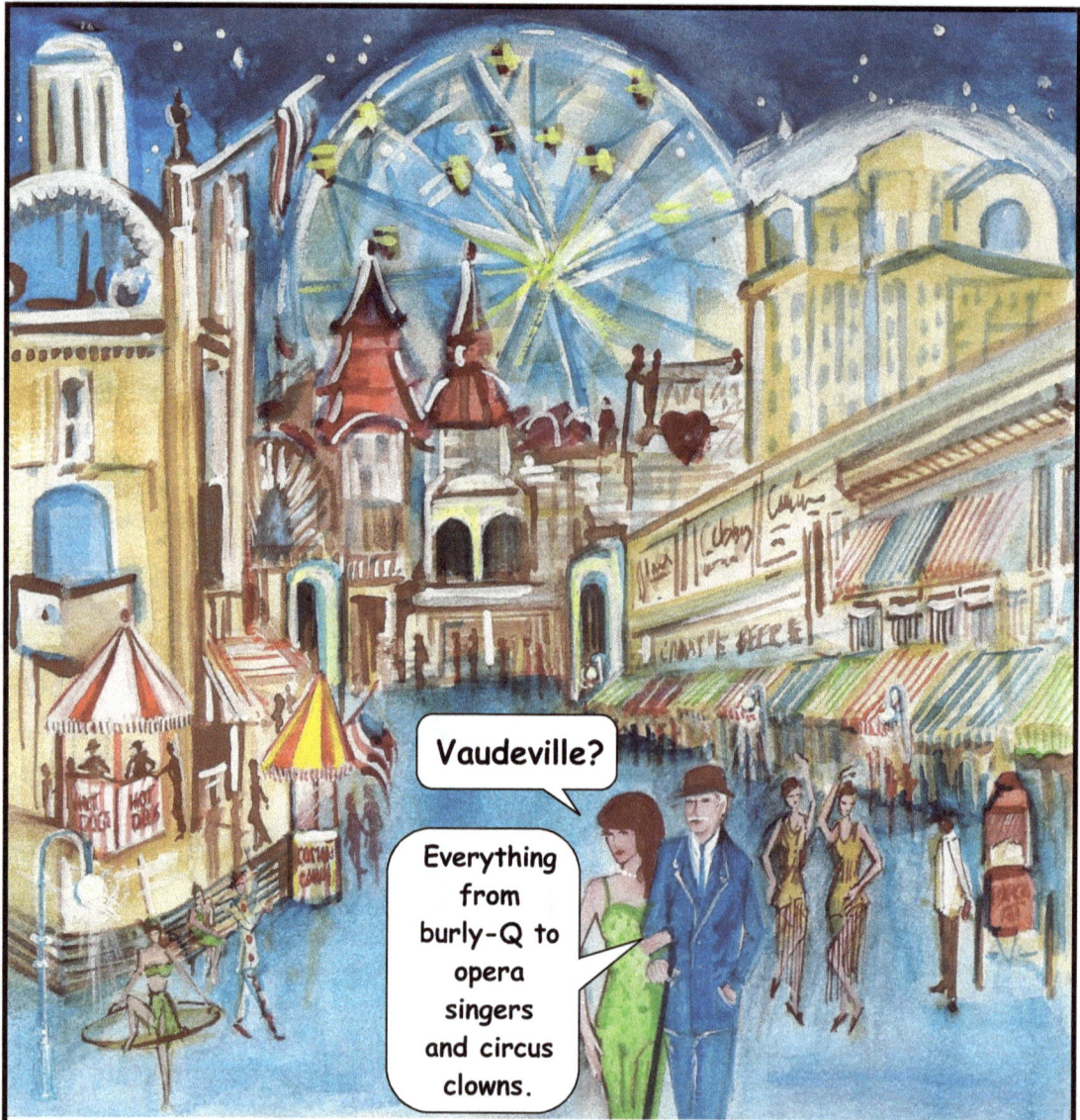

Vaudeville?

Everything from burly-Q to opera singers and circus clowns.

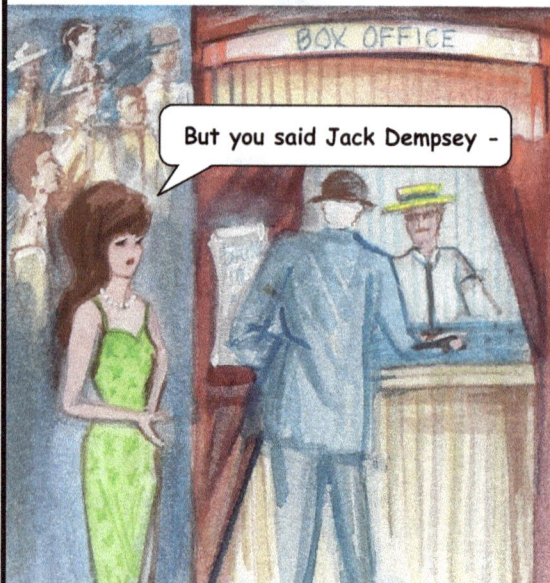

But you said Jack Dempsey -

Clowns of every order.

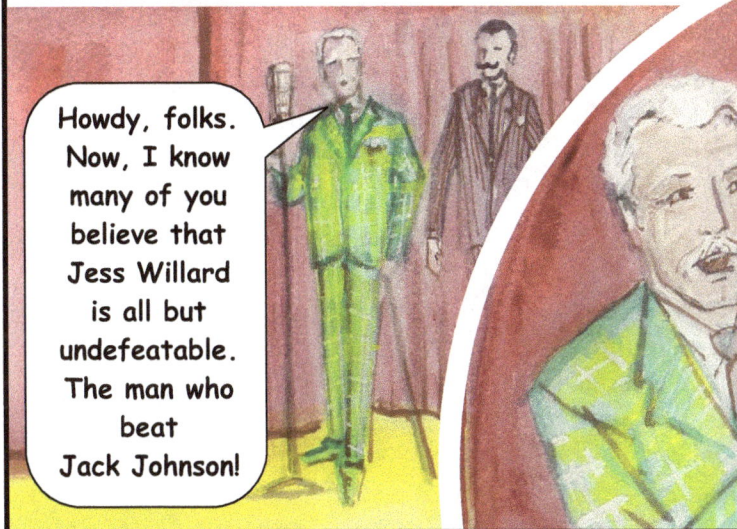

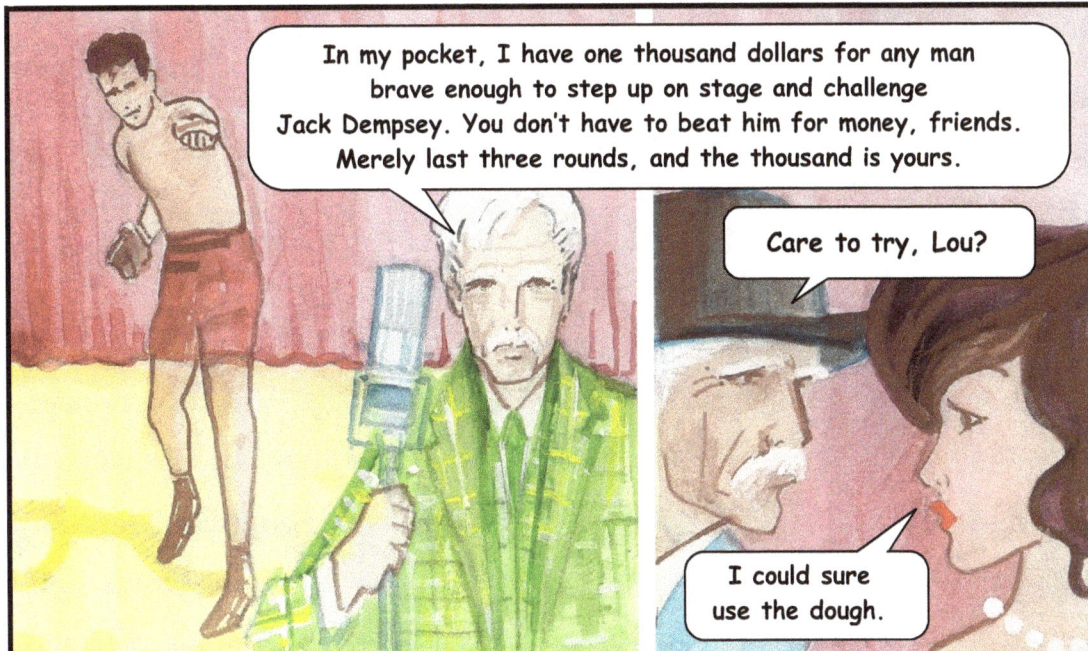

STREAK GOT IN THE FIRST PUNCH, BUT HE DIDN'T CONNECT WITH MAX.

LIKEWISE, WHEN MAX RETURNED THE BLOW.

WHAT HAPPENED NEXT STUNNED THE CROWD.

" WAY BACK WHERE BAT AND I WERE SEATED, WE COULD HEAR THE CRUNCH.'

AND JUST LIKE THAT...

... IT WAS ALL OVER AS QUICK AS IT BEGAN.

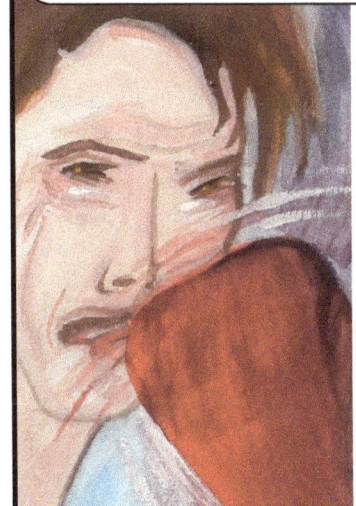

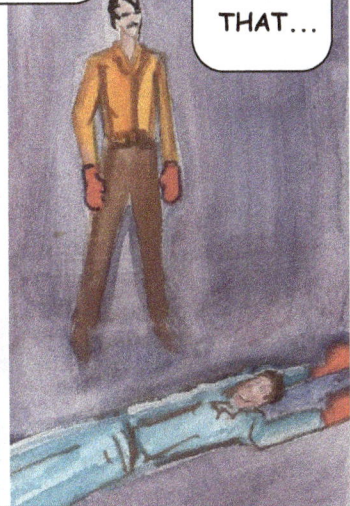

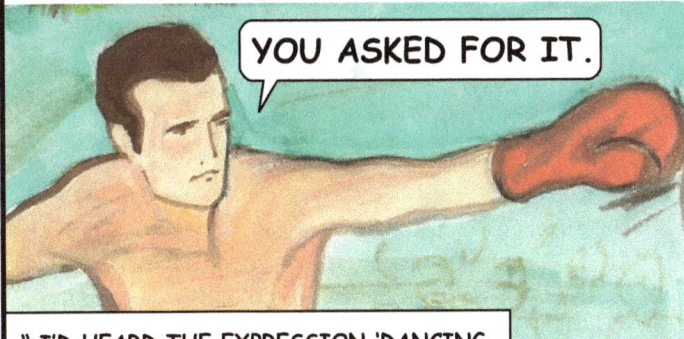

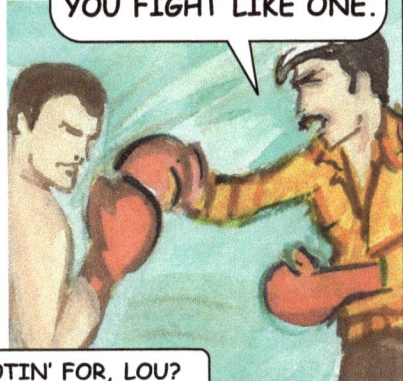

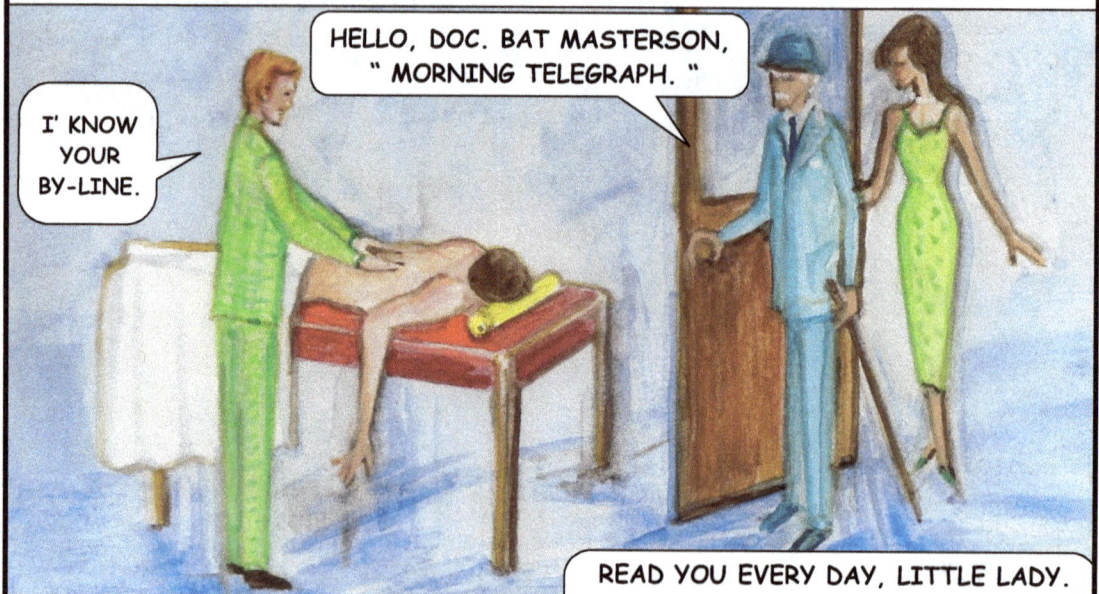

HERE WAS A WORLD I KNEW AS WELL AS BAT
DID THE FRONTIER FROM HIS OWN YOUTH.

44

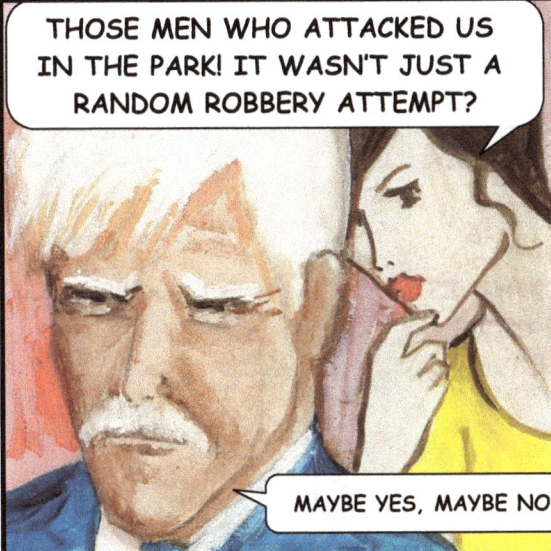

THOSE MEN WHO ATTACKED US IN THE PARK! IT WASN'T JUST A RANDOM ROBBERY ATTEMPT?

MAYBE YES, MAYBE NO.

ROTHSTEIN! YOU DON'T THINK HE'D HAVE ME... KILLED... TO KEEP WHAT I SAW OUT OF THE PAPER?

I TOLD YOU, LOU. THIS IS DANGEROUS STUFF...

IT IS EXCITING, THOUGH. I MEAN, JUST LIKE IN THE MOVIES!

JUST REMEMBER, LOU. THIS IS REAL LIFE. WHERE THINGS DON'T ALWAYS HAVE A HAPPY ENDING.

" HARD AS IT IS TO BELIEVE, I SLEPT SOUNDLY THAT NIGHT. EVEN THOUGH I'D JUST BRUSHED UP AGAINST A WORLD OF BIG MONEY, VAST POWER, AND ABIDING EVIL..."

"...I SLEPT SOUNDLY BECAUSE I KNEW BAT WAS THERE TO GUARD ME. LIKE SOME NOBLE KNIGHT OUT OF AN ARTHURIAN ROMANCE, DUTY BOUND TO PROTECT ELAINE, THE FAIR MAID OF ASTOLAT, READY FOR ANYTHING."

IS ... ANYONE TO HOME?

COME IN, WHOEVER YOU ARE.

IF YOU'VE COME FOR THE RENT, I CAN'T -

JUST GOES TO SHOW: LEAVE THE DOOR UNLOCKED AND NO TELLIN' WHAT MAY WALTZ IN.

I'M SORRY TO DISTURB YOU -

THAT'S NOT WHY I'M HERE.

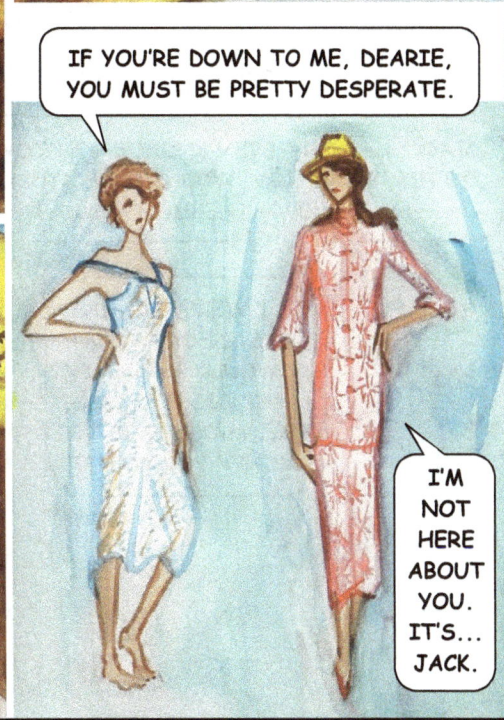

IF YOU'RE DOWN TO ME, DEARIE, YOU MUST BE PRETTY DESPERATE.

MY SOCIAL CALENDAR WAS FREE TODAY.

I'M LOUELLA PARSONS. I WRITE ABOUT CELEBRITIES FOR THE MORNING NEWSPAPER.

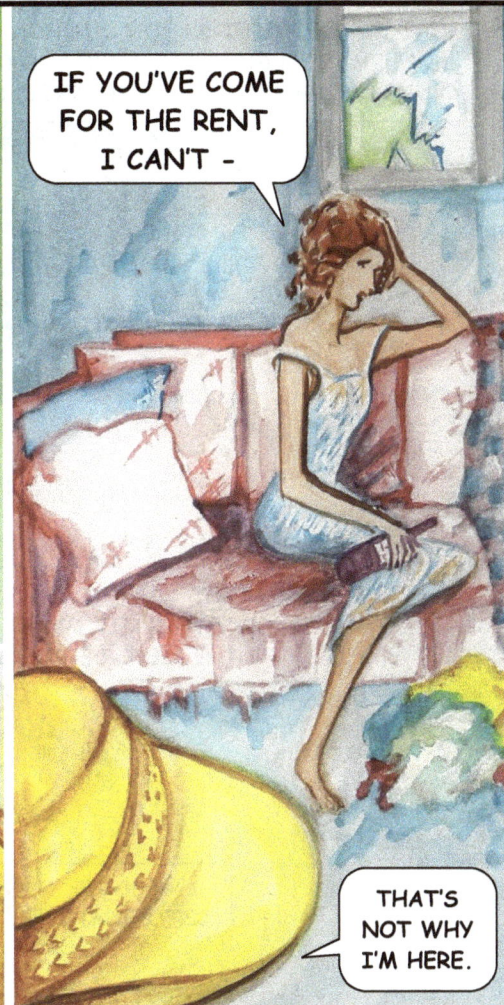

I'M NOT HERE ABOUT YOU. IT'S... JACK.

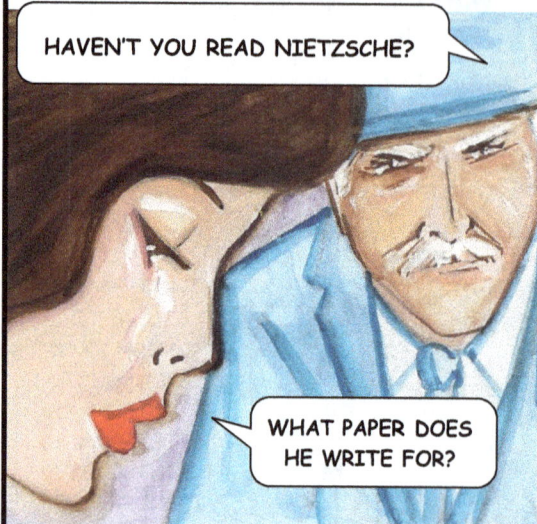

FOR THINE IS THE KINGDOM AND THE POWER FOREVER, AMEN.

IT'S PRECISELY THE POINT. LOOK AT THESE PEOPLE, BAT. SIX DAYS A WEEK, THEY SCURRY ABOUT, EKING OUT A LIVING. THEY NEED SOMETHING TO SUSTAIN THEM. A LITTLE BEAUTY AND MEANING IN THERE LIVES. THIS IS WHERE THEY FIND IT.

I CAN'T DENY THAT.

SEE? I ...

MAYBE. BUT IT'S THE MODERN WAY. AND WHAT DO YOU THINK THEY ALL DO NOW? WHERE DO THEY GO WHEN CHURCH IS OVER?

KARL MARX CLAIMED THAT RELIGION IS THE OPIATE OF THE MASSES.

WHAT A TERRIBLE WAY TO LOOK AT IT!

LET'S FIND OUT. COME ON. WE'LL FOLLOW THE CROWD.

70

BAT? IT WASN'T THAT BAD.

ARRRRRRGH!

THEY GOT IT ALL WRONG!

C'MON. IT'S ONLY A MOVIE.

THOSE PEOPLE IN THERE? THEY'LL BELIEVE WHAT THEY JUST SAW IS THE TRUTH.

WELL, IT IS TRUE YOU SHOT DOWN BADMEN.

YES, LOU. I DID. IT WAS THEM OR ME. I MADE CERTAIN IT WAS THEM. I TOOK NO PLEASURE IN IT, NOR DO I FEEL SHAME NOW. STILL, SOMETHING IN ME DIED EVERY TIME I WAS FORCED TO SHOOT TO KILL. THEY DIDN'T SHOW THAT ONSCREEN. NO BLOOD. ONLY BATHOS.

YOU'RE TALKING ABOUT REALITY. PEOPLE DON'T GO TO THE MOVIES FOR THAT. THEY GET ENOUGH EVERY DAY. WHEN THEY HEAD FOR A THEATER, THEY WANT SOMETHING GLORIOUS.

SOUNDS LIKE YOU'RE TALKING ABOUT CHURCH AGAIN.

COME ON. I'LL SHOW YOU.

MAYBE, IN A WAY, I AM. CHURCH AND THE MOVIES ARE MY TWO FAVORITE PLACES. WHERE WOULD ORDINARY PEOPLE GO WITHOUT THEM?

" FOR THE NEXT FORTY MINUTES, I SAID NOT A WORD. NOR DID MR. ROTHENSTEIN, OR THAT MEAN LOOKING DRIVER UP FRONT. "

" MY GUESS IS THAT WE WERE SOMEWHERE FAR OUT ON LONG ISLAND."

" THANK GOODNESS I HAD THE DERRINGER BAT BOUGHT FOR ME. IF I WERE GOING DOWN, I WAS GOING DOWN FIGHTING! "

I HOPE YOU LIKE SURPRISES.

MAY I TAKE YOUR WRAP, MISS PARSONS?

SAY, YOU'RE LOUELLA PARSONS! THANKS FOR ALL THE NICE MENTIONS IN YOUR COLUMN.

MR. CHAPLIN! I ... I --

PLEASE CALL ME CHARLIE! IF THE WHOLE WORLD DOES, SO CAN THE MOST INFLUENTIAL WRITER IN NEW YORK.

SORRY THAT MY CALL SOUNDED SO FRANTIC. I HAD TO BE CERTAIN YOU'D COME.

MAXINE!

AS LONG AS YOU'RE ALRIGHT.

OH, I'M FINE NOW...

I AM NOW IN GREAT SHAPE!

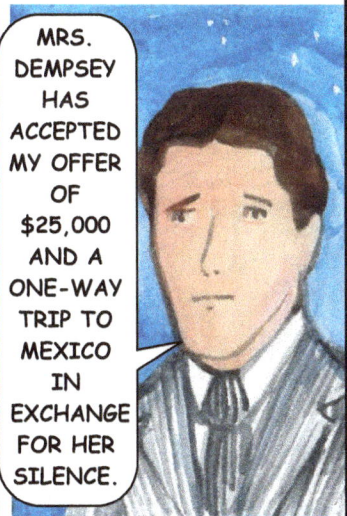

MRS. DEMPSEY HAS ACCEPTED MY OFFER OF $25,000 AND A ONE-WAY TRIP TO MEXICO IN EXCHANGE FOR HER SILENCE.

GOT TO CATCH MY RIDE TO THE AIRPORT. THANK YOU BOTH FOR EVERYTHING!

NOW IF I CAN ONLY PERSUADE YOU TO MAKE NO MENTION OF MAXINE IN YOUR COLUMN, WHILE BUILDING UP JACK'S WHOLESOME REPUTATION ---

YOU ASK A GREAT DEAL OF ME, MR. HEARST.

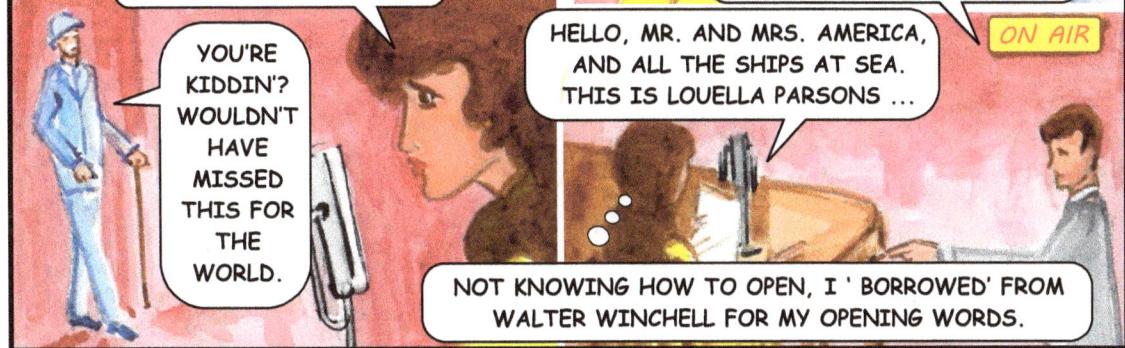

... THERE WAS ONLY ONE BOOK; THE LIFE OF JOHN L. SULLIVAN. MOM BECAME CONVINCED THE CHILD SHE WAS CARRYING WOULD GROW UP TO BE JUST LIKE HIM.

SHE TORE OUT A PICTURE OF HIM AND HUNG IT ON THE WALL.

WORKED IN SHIPYARDS. I'D APPLIED TO THE ARMY BUT WASN'T SELECTED BECAUSE I WAS MY MOTHER'S SOLE SUPPORT.

THIS IS RING LARDNER. DEMPSEY, WHAT DID YOU DO DURING THE WAR?

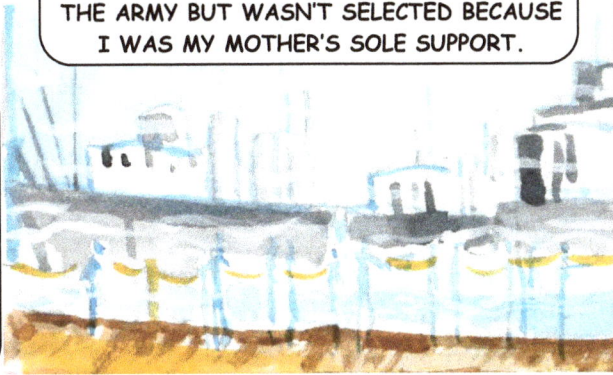

THERE ARE THOSE WHO FEEL THAT THE TITLE SHOT SHOULD GO TO A COMBAT VETERAN.

I BELIEVE THAT HONOR OUGHT TO GO TO THE BEST BOXER. THAT'S ME.

BOTH THOSE MEN ARE COLORED. MR' DEMPSEY, IF YOU WIN THE TITLE, WOULD YOU THEN ACCEPT A CHALLENGE FROM A NEGRO?

I'M JACK LONDON. DO THE NAMES GEORGE CHRISTIAN AND BOSTON BEARCAT RING A BELL WITH YOU?

I FOUGHT BOTH OF THEM. BEAT'EM TOO.

98

YES I AM! BUT IF I WERE TO BE THE REPRESENTATIVE WRITER FOR WOMEN OF THE 1920'S, THEN I HAD TO BE YOUNG.
AND HARRIET? SHE'S NOT SOME STREET WAIF I ADOPTED. SHE'S MY DAUGHTER. I'M DIVORCED FROM A LOSER WHO GAVE ME NOTHING BUT THAT BEAUTIFUL CHILD.
STILL LIKE ME NOW, BAT?
LOU, AT THIS MOMENT I LIKE YOU MORE THAN EVER.
TELL ME FIRST, LOU. IF YOU'RE JEWISH, WHY TELL PEOPLE YOU'RE CATHOLIC?
BECAUSE AS THICK AND HORRIBLE AS PREJUDICE IS TOWARD CATHOLICS IN THIS CITY, IT'S ONE HUNDRED TIMES WORSE TOWARDS JEWS. OBVIOUSLY, I COULDN'T PASS MYSELF OFF AS ANGLO -
MAYBE THIS HAS SOMETHING TO DO WITH WHY I ADMIRE DEMPSEY SO MUCH. HE'S VERY MUCH LIKE ME, YOU KNOW.
HOW SO?
JACK DIDN'T CARE MUCH FOR THE PERSON HE WAS BORN. BUT HE REFUSED TO ACCEPT HIS LOT IN LIFE. SO HE DECIDED TO DO SOMETHING ABOUT IT.
I SEE.
LIKE JACK, I RECREATED MYSELF IN THE IMAGE OF A PERSON I'D BEEN IMAGINING IN MY MIND FOR SOME TIME.
I GUESS MAYBE WE ALL DO THAT.
EVEN YOU? THE GREAT BAT MASTERSON?
MY GIVEN NAME IS BARTHOLOMEW.

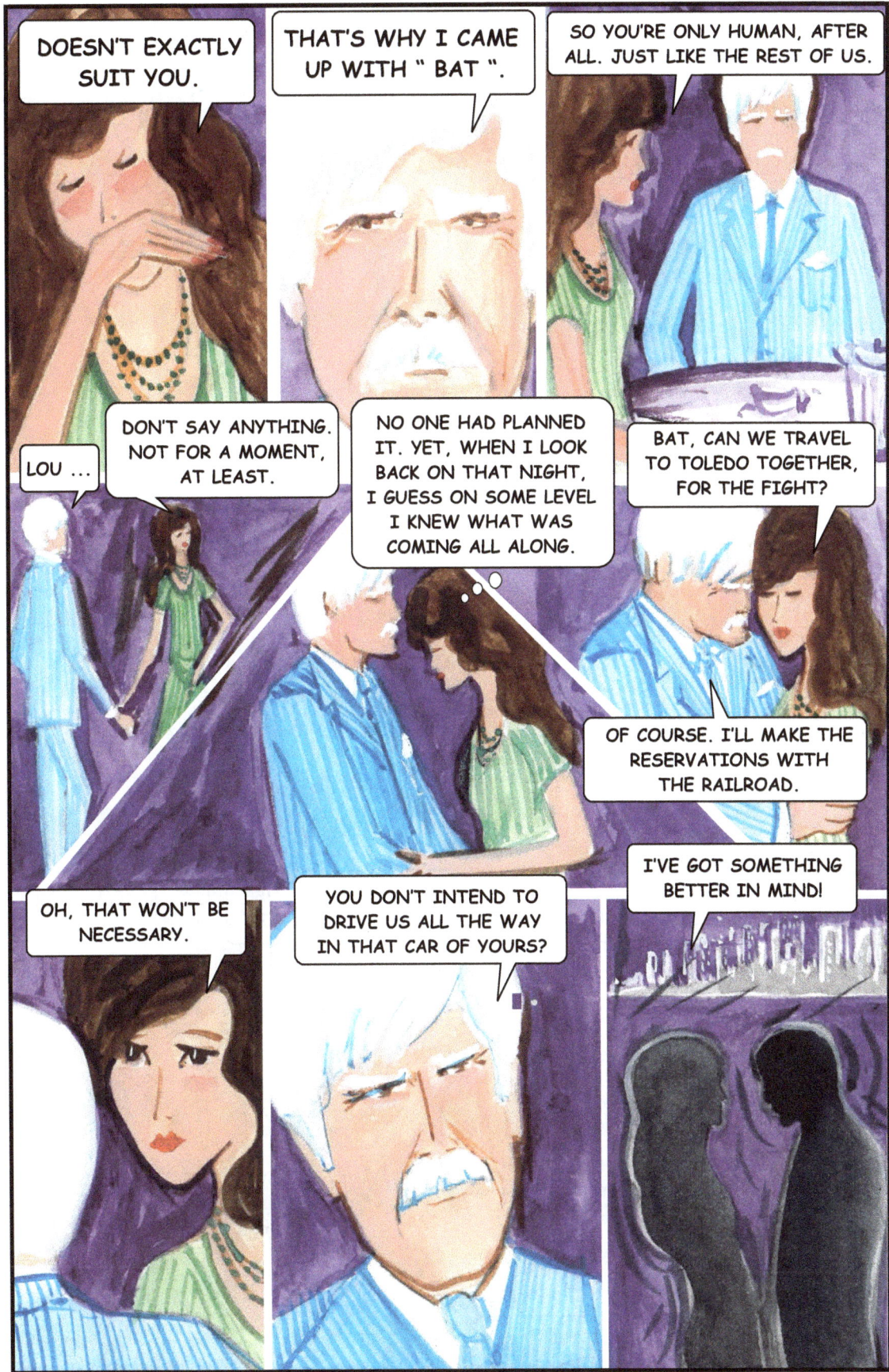

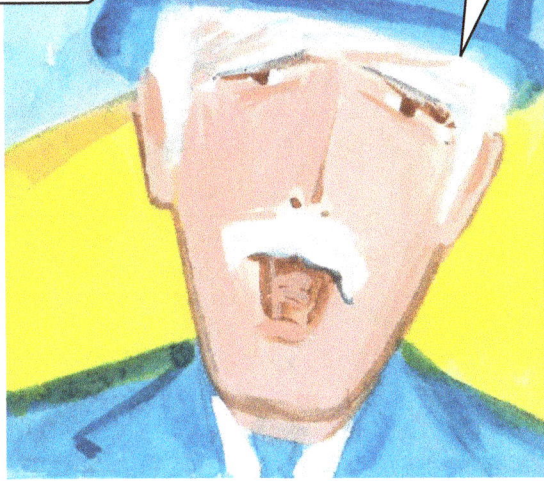

YOU'VE HEARD OF 'EM?

I DO KNOW ABOUT MORE THINGS THAN JUST THE MOVIES. WHY ARE THEY HERE?

I DON'T KNOW, BUT I'M GOING TO FIND OUT.

" IF ANYONE COULD, BAT WAS THE MAN FOR THAT JOB. "

" THE NEXT MORNING, OUR FIRST STOP WAS THE COLISEUM, OR WHAT WAS TO BE THE COLISEUM, IF ONLY FIGHT PROMOTER TEX RICKARD'S WORKERS COULD COMPLETE IT ON TIME. "

NOTHING BUT THE BEST, BAT. WHAT YOU SEE IS THE FINEST LUMBER AVAILABLE.

DO YOU REALLY BELIEVE A HUNDRED THOUSAND PEOPLE WILL SHOW?

THEY WILL IF RAILROADS WILL ADD SOME EXTRA CARS TO THEIR TRAINS, AS IS THE REGULAR ARE ALREADY FULL AND PLENTY OF PEOPLE HAVE NO WAY TO GET HERE.

YOU'RE REALLY COMING TO ENJOY THE POWERS OF THE PRESS, AREN'T YOU, LOU?

I'LL MENTION THAT IN TOMORROW'S COLUMN. THEN BELIEVE ME, THEY WILL SCHEDULE EXTRA PASSENGER CARS. BE CERTAIN: IF THERE'S ONE THING THE RAILROADS HATE, IT'S NEGATIVE PUBLICITY.

WHAT IN THE NAME OF HEAVEN ARE THE LEATHERNECKS DOING HERE?

THE OHIO MINISTERIAL ASSOCIATION WAS TRYING TO SHUT DOWN THE FIGHT. CLAIMED BOXING ISN'T CHRISTIAN. BUT ONE OF MY INVESTORS IS A.J.D. BIDDLE, A BUSINESSMAN WHO MAKES BIG CONTRIBUTIONS TO BIBLE CLASSES. HE HUSHED THEM DOWN WITH A HEFTY ENDOWMENT. BUT ONLY IF I WOULD AGREE TO LET THE U.S. MARINES PERFORM PREVIOUS TO THE FIGHT. BIDDLE WS A MAJOR IN THE WAR AND HE LOVES TO SHOW THESE BOYS OFF BEFORE A BIG CROWD.

SEEMS LIKE THERE'S MORE THAN ONE BIG BATTLE TAKING PLACE HERE.

" NEXT STOP WAS JESS WILLARD'S TRAINING CAMP. I'D NEVER MET HIM AND, WHATEVER MY PERSONAL LOYALTIES WERE, I WAS EXCITED ABOUT BEING INTRODUCED TO THE REIGNING HEAVYWEIGHT CHAMPION. "

SHOULDN'T WILLARD BE SPARRING?

YUP. LET'S FIND OUT WHY HE'S NOT.

MASTERSON? COME ON IN. HEY! NO WOMEN ALLOWED.

THIS IS LOUELLA PARSONS. YOU KNOW: THE COLUMNIST?

YEAH? WE'LL MAKE AN EXCEPTION.

WE WERE SURPRISED NOT TO FIND YOU OUT IN THE RING, JESS.

WHEN I ARRIVED, I LEARNED THAT THE DOWNY QUILT THAT GOT TO BE PLACED BENEATH THE RING HADN'T ARRIVED..

SOON AS THEY'RE DELIVERED, I'LL START TRAINING.

YOU COULD BE JUMPING ROPE, OR RUNNING. DOESN'T YOUR MANAGER ...

WHAT MANAGER?

YOU DON'T HAVE ONE?

TO FIGHT SOME LITTLE GNAT? HA! WHO NEEDS ONE?

THEN COMES MY FAVORITE TIME OF THE DAY. LUNCH! BAT WAS AS SURPRISED AS ME BY AN UNEXPECTED BUT WELCOME VISITOR.

WELCOME "FIGHT CITY!"

WELCOME "FIGHT CITY"

HELLO, BAT. IT'S BEEN A MONTH OF SUNDAYS. MAY I JOIN YOU?

AM I SEEING THINGS OR IS THAT REALLY YOU, WYATT?

WHEN WAS THE LAST TIME WE WERE TOGETHER? DODGE CITY? TOMBSTONE?

ARE YOU... REALLY... ACTUALLY...

LOU, MEET MY OLDEST AND BEST FRIEND: WYATT EARP. THE MAN WHO TAUGHT ME EVERYTHING I KNOW.

TRUE! THEN AGAIN, I DIDN'T TEACH HIM ALL I KNOW.

I'M LOUELLA PARSONS.

THE JOURNALIST!

THE PAPER SENT ME TO COVER THE FIGHT FROM A PERSONALITY ANGLE. GOSSIP FOR YOUNG WOMEN READERS WHO HAVE GONE QUITE MAD FOR JACK DEMPSEY.

AND I'M CONCENTRATING ON THE SPORT. WHAT BRINGS YOU HERE, WYATT?

BELIEVE IT OR NOT, THE OFFICIALS BROUGHT ME OUT OF RETIREMENT TO SERVE AS A TEMPORARY DEPUTY. KEEP THINGS CALM AND QUIET ON THE DAY OF THE BIG FIGHT.

WHY, THE TWO OF YOU TOGETHER AGAIN IS ... WELL .... HISTORICAL!.

HUH! JUST LIKE OLD TIMES.

110

THERE WAS NO HARD EVIDENCE TO PROVE WHO KILLED THOSE KLANSMAN. THE LOCALS PLAYED IT DOWN AS MUCH AS POSSIBLE SO AS NOT TO TARNISH THE BIG EVENT WHICH THEY HOPED WOULD PUT TOLEDO ON THE MAP. I KEPT FILING MY PRE-FIGHT STORIES. THEN, TWO NIGHTS BEFORE THE BIG EVENT ...

IN THE FIRST PLACE, I'VE NEVER BEEN IN BRIMSTONE IN MY LIFE.

I KNOW, YOU TWO TAMED DODGE. BUT THERE WERE SOME BEAUTIFUL LOCATIONS WE COULD CAPTURE WITH THE CAMERA IF ONLY WE CHANGED THE SETTING.

AND THE GET-UP YOU HAD US WEARING? NO TRUE WESTERNER EVER SPORTED BIG WHITE HATS LIKE THAT. OR THE JEWELED GUN BELTS AND SILVER SPURS ...

OH, BUT MR. EARP. THE PUBLIC LOVES STUFF LIKE THAT!

BUT YOU GOT ALL THE FACTS WRONG.

IT WAS NOTHING BUT A WIND-BAG LEGEND.

LOOK AT IT THIS WAY: WHEN THE LEGEND BECOMES A FACT, PRINT THE LEGEND.

IS THAT HOLLYWOOD'S CREED?

IT'S MY OWN, I'M JOHN FORD. I MAKE WESTERNS.

" THOUGH THE MATCH WASN'T SCHEDULED TO BEGIN UNTIL FOUR IN THE AFTERNOON, PEOPLE ARRIVED AT THE MAIN GATE BEFORE THE CRACK OF DAWN."

WELCOME TOLEDO TO THE BIG EVENT!

119

LATER, JACK TOLD ME HE HADN'T BEEN ABLE TO SLEEP ALL NIGHT; HE WAS UP AND OUT AT THE CRACK OF DAWN, GETTING IN SOME LAST MINUTE PRACTICE.

REMEMBER, KID. DON'T SHOW NO ANXIETY, NO EMOTION. NO NOTHIN'. REMEMBER THIS: ATTITUDE IS EVERYTHING!

THOUGH BAT AND I HAD BEEN THE FIRST MEMBERS OF THE PRESS TO ARRIVE, WE'D NOW BEEN JOINED BY ...

... RING LARDNER, JACK LONDON, DAMON RUNYON, AND OTHERS FROM NEWSPAPERS AND SYNDICATES. EVIDENTLY, MY COLUMNS HAD WORKED THEIR INTENDED EFFECT: THIS HAD TURNED INTO THE FIGHT OF THE CENTURY!

JESS WILLARD TOOK THE MORNING OFF. HE WAS CERTAIN THAT A LITTLE IRISH PIP-SQUEAK PRESENTED SUCH AN INSIGNIFICANT CHALLENGE THAT IT WASN'T NECESSARY TO OVER' EXERT HIMSELF.

THE PROMOTERS' BIGGEST FEAR WAS THAT SOME OF THE MEN MIGHT GET DRUNK AND DISORDERLY. BUT THERE WOULD BE NO "SERIOUS" VIOLENCE THIS DAY, FOR BAT AND WYATT WERE STATIONED OUT FRONT TO MAKE CERTAIN NO FIREARMS WERE CARRIED INSIDE, JUST AS THEY HAD DONE IN DODGE CITY HALF A CENTURY EARLIER.

NO ONE ENTERS WITHOUT BEING FRISKED FIRST.

YOU WILL SURRENDER ALL GUNS AND KNIVES, THEN PICK'EM UP AS YOU LEAVE.

YEAH? AND WHO THE HELL ARE YOU?

WILLIAM BARTLEY MASTERSON. CALL ME BAT.

I"M WYATT EARP.

THAT MEANT SOMETHING ONCE. NOT NOW.

LET ME DISPROVE THAT THEORY.

SO YOU'RE THE FAMOUS MARSHAL WHO BROUGHT IN IKE CLANTON, JOHNNY RINGO, AND CURLY BILL?

CORRECT, NOW, IT'S YOUR TURN.

HOW MANY YEARS SINCE WE DID LAST THAT?

MORE THAN I CARE TO REMEMBER!

BY 10:30 AM, THE HEAT HAD RISEN TO 106 . THE FAINT OF HEART WERE ALREADY PASSING OUT; WITHIN A FEW HOURS, THE STRONGER FOLKS WOULD BE JOINING THEM UNLESS THEY SHELLED OUT FOR AN UMBRELLA TO SHADE THEMSELVES FROM THE SUN. RICKARD'S FRESH NEW WOOD TURNED OUT TO BE A DISASTER, AS THE PLANK BLEACHERS OOSED SAP; THOSE WITH THE CASH TO PAY FOR CUSHIONS SAVED THE SEATS OF THEIR PANTS FROM BEING RUINED. THE OTHERS? WELL, THAT WAS THEIR TOUGH LUCK. BY NOON, ALL THE COLD BEVERAGES AND ICE CREAM WERE GONE. THE AUDIENCE, LIKE OUR MODERN GLADIATORS, WERE IN FOR AN ENDURANCE TEST.

THE WOMEN'S SUFFRAGE MOVEMENT SAW THIS AS A PERFECT EVENT TO CAMPAIGN FOR EQUALITY. DESPITE SOME PROTEST, FROM THAT DAY ON, WOMEN WOULD BE ADMITTED TO ALL BOXING MATCHES.

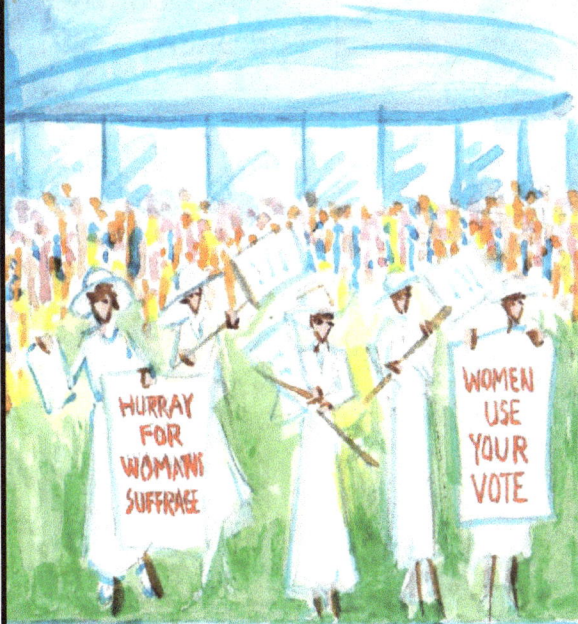

BLACKS ATTENDING THE EVENT WERE SEGREGATED, THOUGH IT COULD HAVE BEEN EVEN WORSE. IN SOME STATES, THEY WOULD HAVE NOT BEEN ALLOWED TO EVEN ATTEND. THOSE WHO WERE HERE TODAY HAD HEARD ABOUT WHAT THE KLAN HAD DONE, AND FIGURED THAT ANYONE DESPISED BY THAT GROUP WAS A HERO TO THEIR CAUSE.

HURRAY FOR WOMAN SUFFRAGE

WOMEN USE YOUR VOTE

BLACKS ONLY

THE KLANSMAN HAD TURNED OUT IN DROVES TO SUPPORT JESS WILLARD. THEY CALLED HIM THEIR GREAT WHITE HOPE. ONCE AGAIN, I WAS FORCED TO REALIZE HOW MANY THINGS THIS SPORTING EVENT MEANT TO DIFFERENT GROUPS OF PEOPLE.

IF THE KLAN PLANNED TO KEEP A CLOSE EYE TRAINED ON THE BLACKS, THEN THE WESTIES WERE WATCHING IN CASE THE KLAN DARED TRY ANYTHING HERE. I SENSED AN UNSPOKEN ALLIANCE FORMING BETWEEN THE BLACKS AND THE BLACK-IRISH.

THE VETERANS WERE THERE TO PROTEST JACK AS HE HADN'T SERVED DURING THE GREAT WAR.

ENJOY IT WHILE YOU CAN. WE JUST PASSED PROHIBITION. THE FIGHT GAME IS NEXT.

OUTSIDE, THE WOMEN'S TEMPERANCE LEAGUE TOOK NO SIDES AS TO THE FIGHT. THEY WERE AGAINST BOXING AND DEMANDED IT BE SHUT DOWN FOR OUR SOCIETY TO BECOME CIVILIZED.

GET OUT OF THE WAY. LEAVE US BE.

NOW, NOW. TEMPER, TEMPER ...

EVERYONE WAS THERE, GOOD AND BAD ALIKE.

THAT'S WHEN I FINALLY MADE MY GRAND ENTRANCE.

I KNEW AT ONCE SOMETHING WAS WRONG.

HI, BAT! WYATT!

HELLO.

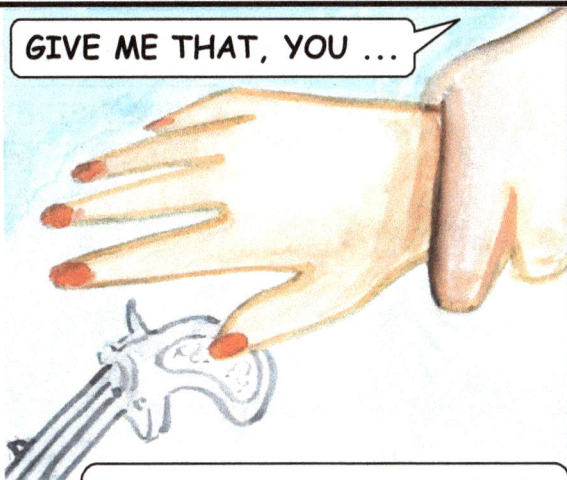

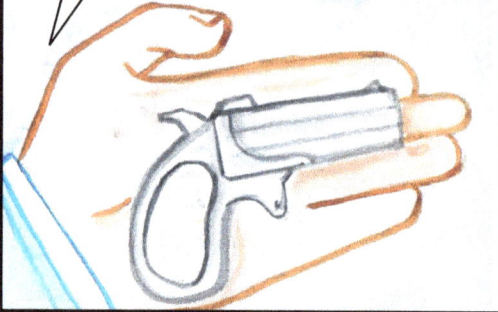

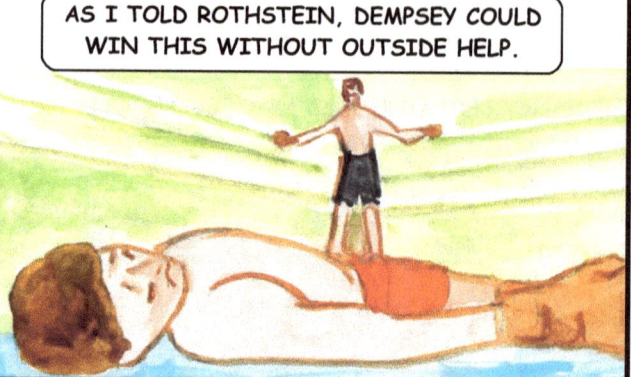

EVERYONE IN THE CROWD NOW KNEW THAT THIS COULD GO EITHER WAY.
THIS IS SO GREAT!
JUST KEEP IN MIND: IT'S FAR FROM OVER.
AT THIS MOMENT, NO ONE COULD TAKE HIS OR HER EYES OFF THE RING.
WHICH OUR OLD ACQUAINTANCE, PETER THE PAINTER, HAD BEEN COUNTING ON.
BEFORE THAT FIRST ROUND WAS OVER, JACK HAD KNOCKED WILLARD DOWN SIX MORE TIMES.
JACK MOVED LIKE A JUNGLE CAT, FAST AND POWERFUL.
WHILE WILLARD BEGAN TO LOOK LIKE A FLESH AND BLOOD PUNCHING BAG.
ONE ... TWO ... THREE ...

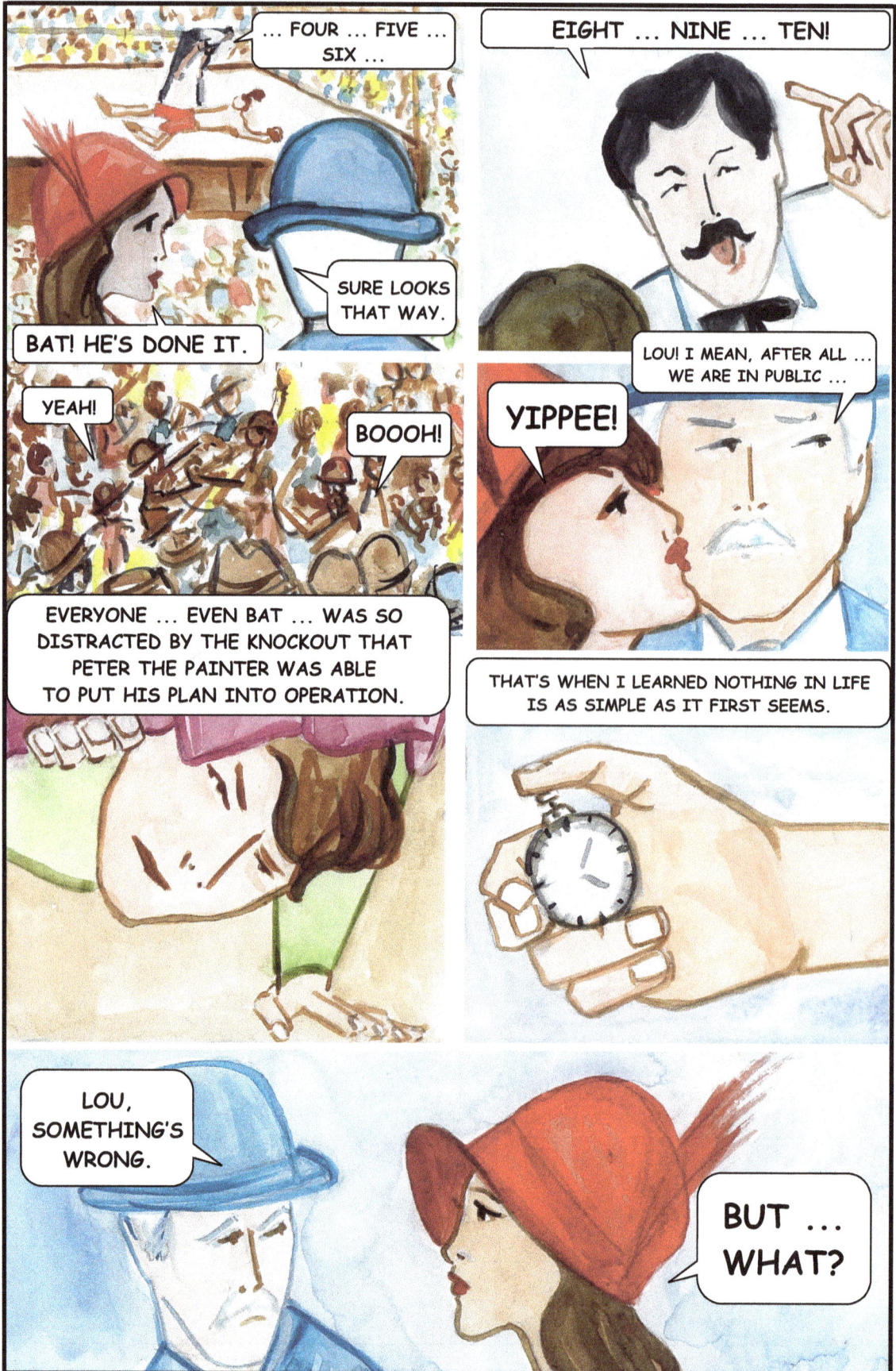

GO AHEAD. NAME ME THE WINNER!

STOP HIM, ANY WAY YOU CAN. I'LL LOOK FOR WHATEVER THE PAINTER SET UNDER THE RING.

MAYBE I'M GETTIN' A LITTLE OLD FOR THIS KIND OF STUFF.

LOOK. HE'S IN!

THERE WAS PLENTY TO WORRY ABOUT UP TOP AS WELL.

IT'S A MAZE UNDER HERE. WHERE TO LOOK FIRST?

THAT'S CUTTIN' IT CLOSE, BOYS.

"DING"

THIS TIME, MR. ROTHSTEIN, I WILL SHOOT IF YOU DON'T DROP THAT AT ONCE.

OW!

IF WILLARD RECOVERS AND BEATS DEMPSEY, EVERYTHING THAT MR. HEARST PROMISED YOU IS GONE!

I KNOW THAT. BUT LIKE JACK, I WANT TO WIN FAIR AND SQUARE OR NOT AT ALL.

IN THE RING, JACK WAS DOING PRECISELY THAT.

AHA!

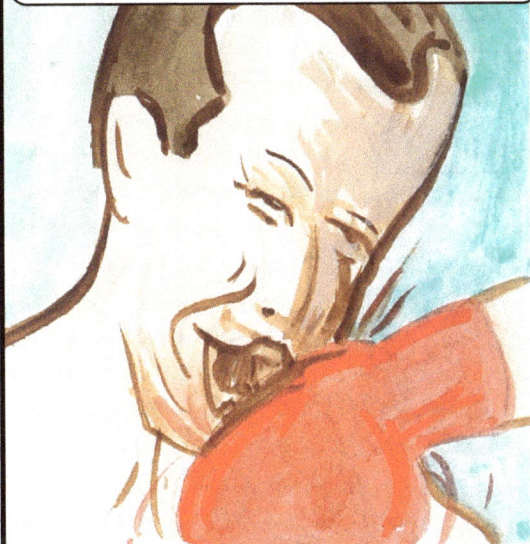

143

144

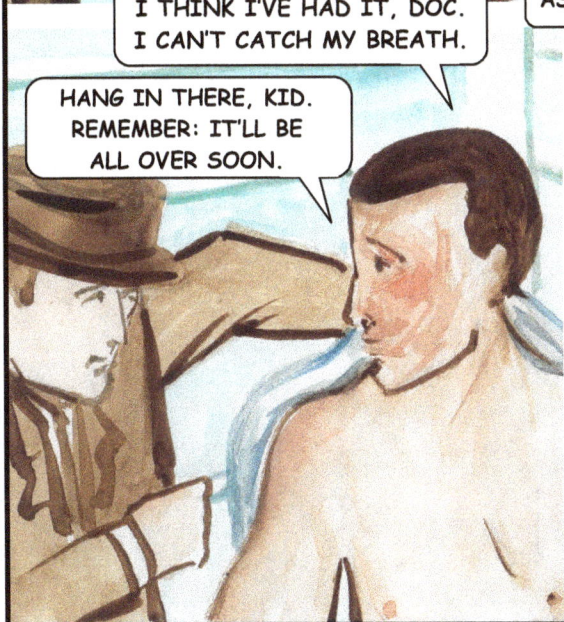

I NEVER SAW BAT AGAIN. HOLLYWOOD BECKONED TO ME, WHILE HE WAS BACK IN NEW YORK. WE DID SPEAK SEVERAL TIMES ON THE PHONE. ALWAYS, I WOULD PROMISE TO RETURN FOR A VISIT, BUT THERE WAS SO MUCH WORK TO BE DONE.

ON OCTOBER 25, 1921. BAT SUFFERED A HEART ATTACK WHILE AT HIS DESK, TYPING WHAT WOULD BE HIS LAST COLUMN.

MR. LEWIS FOUND THE FOLLOWING WORDS TYPED OUT, THE LAST BAT WOULD WRITE.

" THERE ARE MANY IN THIS WORLD WHO HOLD WE ALL OF US GET THE SAME AMOUNT OF ICE IN LIFE. YES, ONLY THE RICH GET IT IN THE SUMMERTIME, THE POOR IN THE WINTER, SOME SAY THAT THIS PROVES ' THE EQUALITY OF THE CLASSES.' ME? I JUST CAN'T SEE IT THAT WAY."

MR. LEWIS DID WHAT BAT WOULD HAVE WANTED: HE PRINTED THOSE FAMOUS LAST WORDS. BENEATH THEM, APPEARED MR. LEWIS'S OBIT: 'GOODBYE, BAT. WE NEVER HEARD YOU BLAT ABOUT THE THINGS YOU DID OUT WEST. YOU WEREN'T BUILT LIKE THAT.'

HE WAS A MAN OF THE PAST, WHO EMBRACED ALL THE EMERGENT IDEAS. I? A WOMAN FOR THE FUTURE, WHO CLUNG TO OLD PROVINCIAL VALUES. ALL THE SAME, BAT MASTERSON TAUGHT ME MANY THINGS THAT WOULD SUSTAIN ME THROUGH THE YEARS. MOST IMPORTANTLY, HE TAUGHT ME THE VALUE OF SAND.

Character Sketches

Lou
Fashions of the 1920s
Jack Dempsey Fight
Bat and Lou

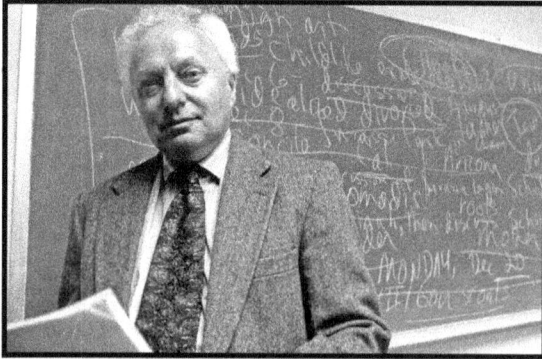

About the Author

DOUGLAS BRODE is a novelist, graphic novelist, playwright, film historian, multi-award winning journalist and multi-award-winning educator. He created and taught the Film Classics program at the Newhouse School of Public Communications, Syracuse University, until his retirement. Among his books for Sunbury Press are The Planet Jesus Trilogy (written with his son, Shaun L. Brode) and the non-fiction novel *PATSY: The Life and Times of Lee Harvey Oswald*. Brode's latest distinction is inclusion in a recent edition of *Who's Who in America*.

About the Illustrator

ROSE MARY CASCIANO MOZIAK is a freelance artist. She received a Bachelor of Fine Arts degree from Syracuse University. Rose Mary lives in Fayetteville, New York, with her husband, Donald, and has two sons, Cristopher and Daniel.

www.ingramcontent.com/pod-product-compliance
Lightning Source LLC
Chambersburg PA
CBHW080045280326

41935CB00014B/1785